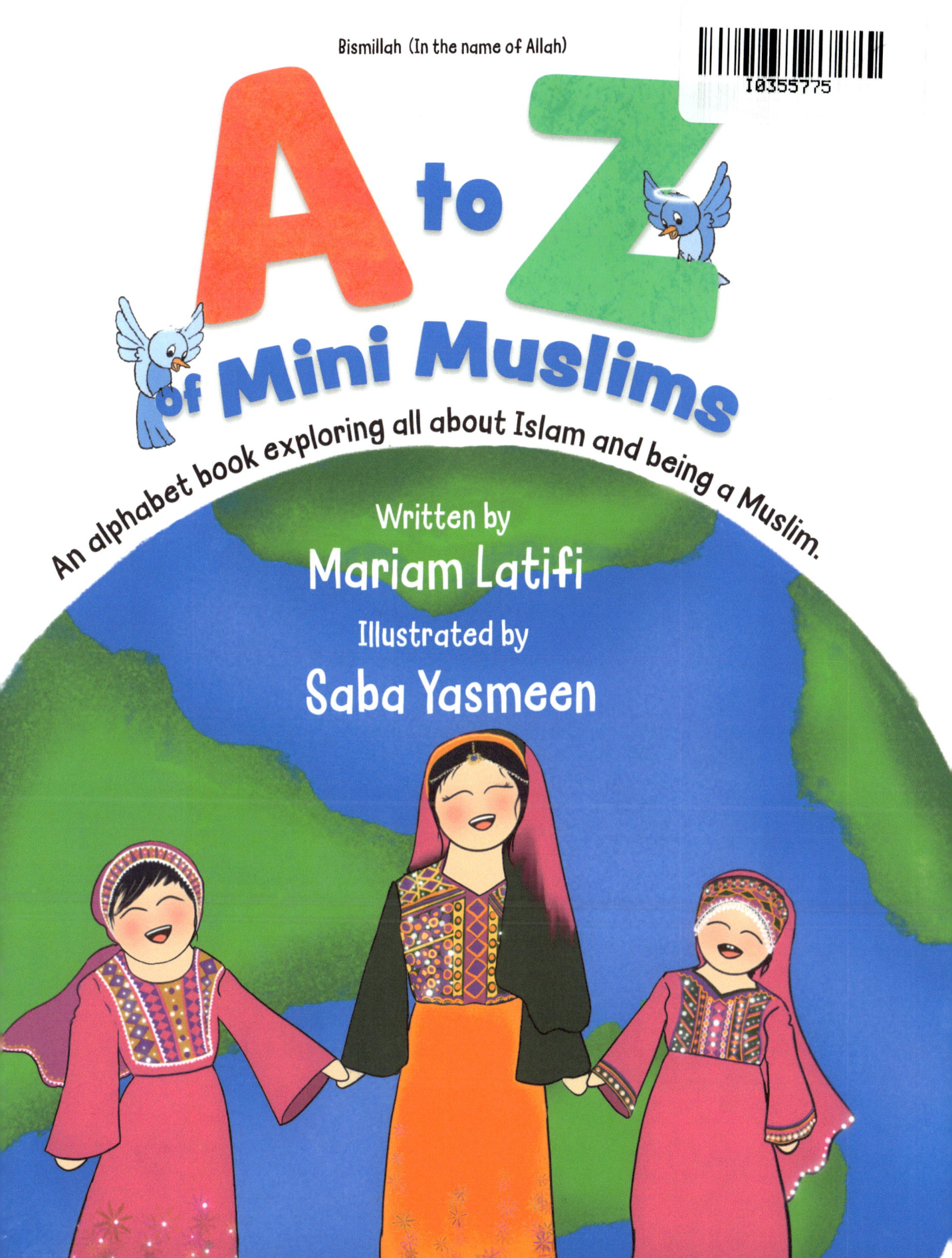

The A to Z of Mini Muslims is a work of fiction. Names, characters, places and incidents are the products of the author's imagination, or used fictitiously. Any resemblance to actual events, locales, businesses, or persons, living or dead, is entirely coincidental.

Copyright © 2021 by Mariam Latifi
Sydney, NSW, Australia

All rights reserved. No part of this book may be reproduced or transmitted in any form or by any means, electronic or mechanical, including photocopying, recording, or by any information and retrieval systems, without the written permission of the copyright owner except for the use of quotations in a book review. For more information, address: latifi.mariam@gmail.com

Illustrated by Saba Yasmeen
Edited by Nilufer Kurtuldu & Jackie Hosking
Book Design by Praise Saflor

ISBN: 978-0-6452720-0-0 (Paperback)
978-0-6452720-1-7 (Hardcover)
978-0-6452720-2-4 (Ebook)

A catalogue record for this book is available from the National Library of Australia

In the spirit of reconciliation the Gift of Knowledge acknowledges the Traditional Custodians of country throughout Australia and their connections to land, sea and community. We pay our respect to their Elders past and present and extend that respect to all Aboriginal and Torres Strait Islander peoples today.

www.mariamlatifi.com.au

Dedication

To my wonderful Mum and Dad and
to all the amazing parents out there!

For my three beautiful girls, Sama, Sana & Safa Wasseh
that have inspired me to write this book.

To my beautiful angel up in heaven,
to God we belong and to Him we will return.

For all the beautiful children reading this book and for
those up in heaven, this book is dedicated to you all.

To all the children of now and of the future.
May knowledge empower you all!

Finally, I dedicate this book in loving memory to
my amazing and inspirational Grandfather Al-Hajj
Mohammad Shafi Haider-Wardak. He was a man of
honour, wisdom, courage and bravery who instilled in us
the love for our religion and education and the power of
justice and respect we should have to all of mankind.

Aa is for Allah SWT

The Almighty, The All-Wise
The One and only true God!

Muslims believe in only one God who created everything.

Cc is for Crescent Moon

That signifies the beginning of the new lunar month.

1. Muharram
2. Safar
3. Rabi' ul-Awwal
4. Rabi' ath-Thani
5. Jumadi al-Awwal
6. Jumadi al-Thani
7. Rajab
8. Sha'ban
9. Ramadan
10. Shawwal
11. Dhu al-Qa'dah
12. Dhu al-Hijjah

There are 12 Islamic months in the Year.

Dd is for Dua

We ask Allah for whatever our hearts desire.

O Allah! Please protect my family and I and bless us with good health, imaan and success. We love you Allah! Thank you for everything!

O Allah! I ask You for your forgiveness. I may have done wrong, but I want to come back to You and repent.

A Muslim festivity and celebration. A time in which everyone comes together to celebrate. Muslims celebrate Eid twice a year. Eid-ul-Fitr (feast of breaking the fast) and Eid-ul-Adha (feast of sacrifice).

Hh is for Hajj

A journey to Makkah, the 5th pillar of Islam.

Day 1 — Perform tawaf → Safa → perform sa'i → Marwa

Day 2 — Depart from Mina → Mount Arafah → Make dua and pray

Day 3 — Spend night at Muzdalifah → Jamarat → Animal sacrifice and trim hair

Day 4-6 — Return to Kaaba for Tawaf and Sa'i → Farewell tawaf

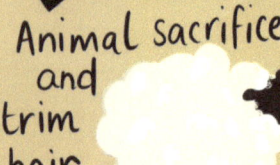

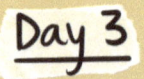

Ii is for Islam

Which means submission to the will of Allah.

Our beautiful religion of peace,
that teaches us to be kind to all.

Jj is for Jannah

Which means Paradise.
A beautiful place that we hope to enter.

We have to work hard and earn lots of good deeds to be able to enter this.

Ll is for Laylat al-Qadr

Which means the "Night of Power".

A most wonderful night better than a 1000 months.

Ramadan

1	2	3	4	5	6	7
8	9	10	11	12	13	14
15	16	17	18	19	20	**21**
22	**23**	24	**25**	26	**27**	28
29	30

It falls on one of the odd nights of the last 10 days of Ramadan. This was the night that the Quran was revealed.

Mm is for Prophet Mohammad
(Sallallahu Alayhi Wa Sallam)

Our final Prophet in Islam,
who was sent with the holy Quran.

Oo is for Obey

Where we follow Allah's commands. We follow what is acceptable (Halal) and avoid what is forbidden (Haram).

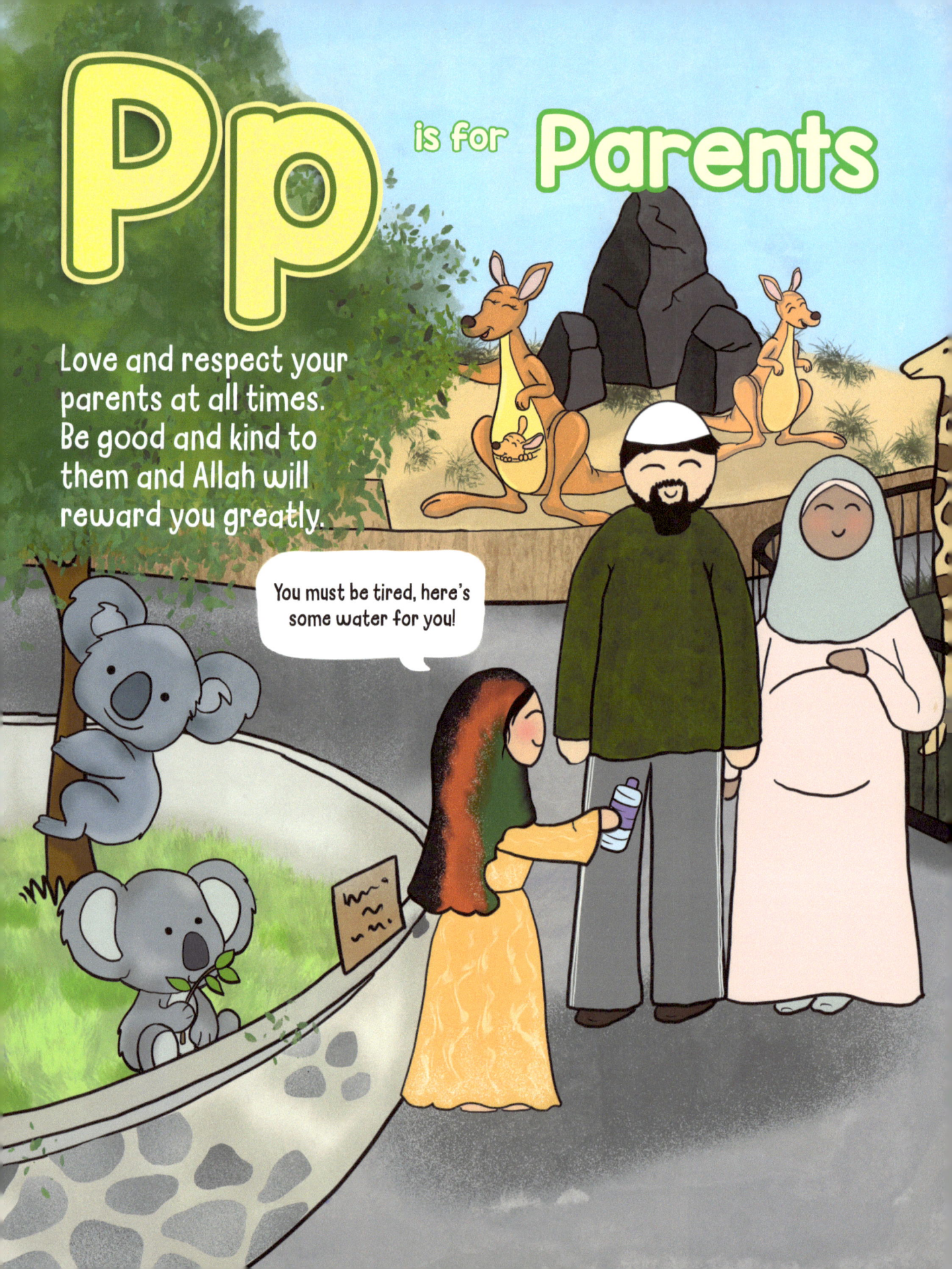

Qq is for Quran

The words of Allah, which was sent to the Prophet Mohammad (Sallallahu Alayhi Wa Sallam) to teach mankind.

Rr is for Ramadan

The 9th month of the Islamic Lunar Calendar.
The holy month of fasting for Muslims all around the world.

Dhikr

Taraweeh

Read

Fasting

Du'a

Ss is for Salah

Which we pray five times a day.
From Fajr (dawn), Dhuhr (midday), Asr (afternoon), Maghrib (sunset) to Isha (night).

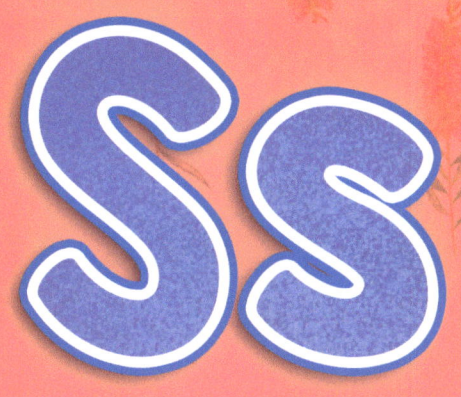

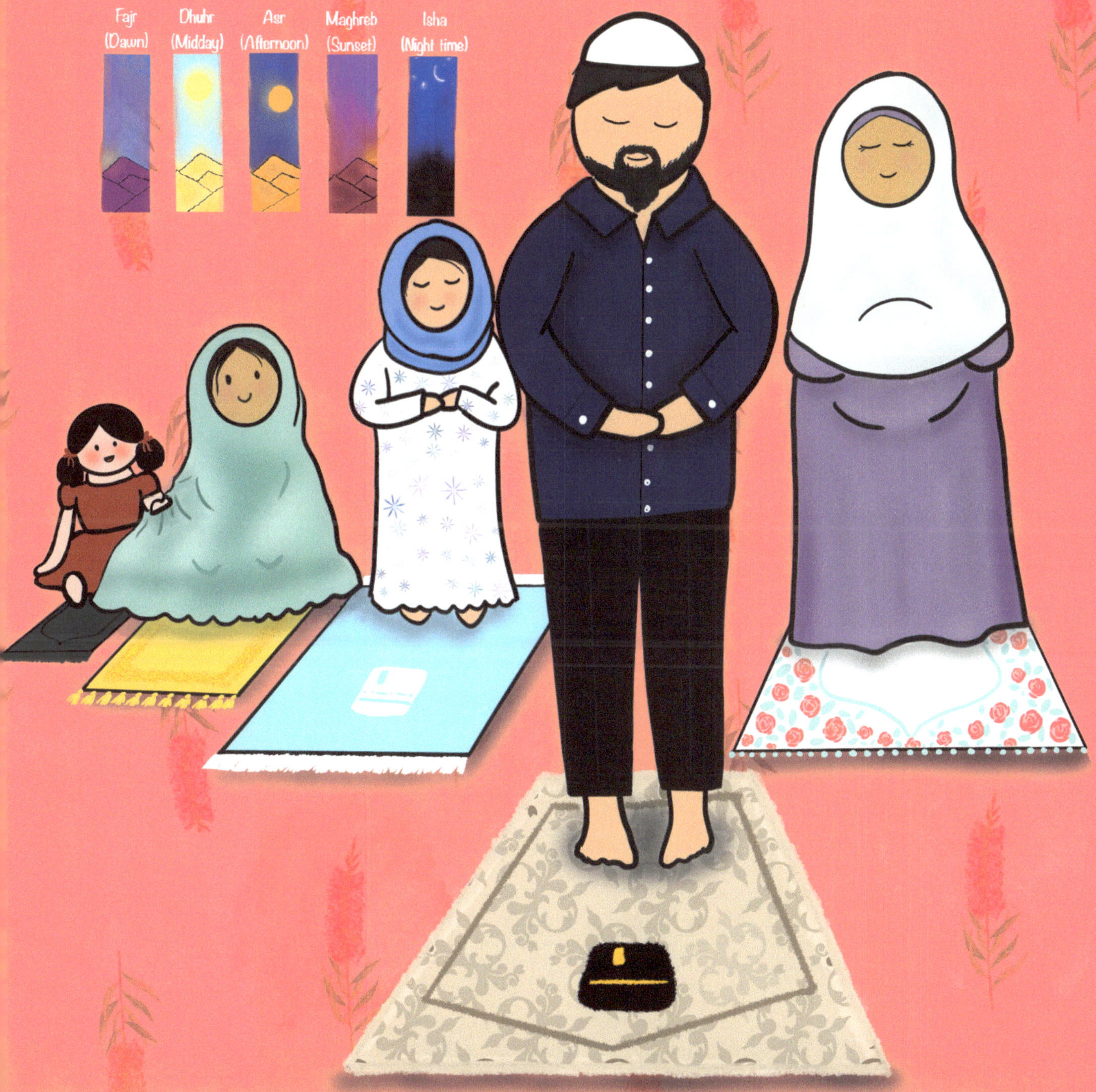

Tt is for Taharah

Which means purity and cleanliness.

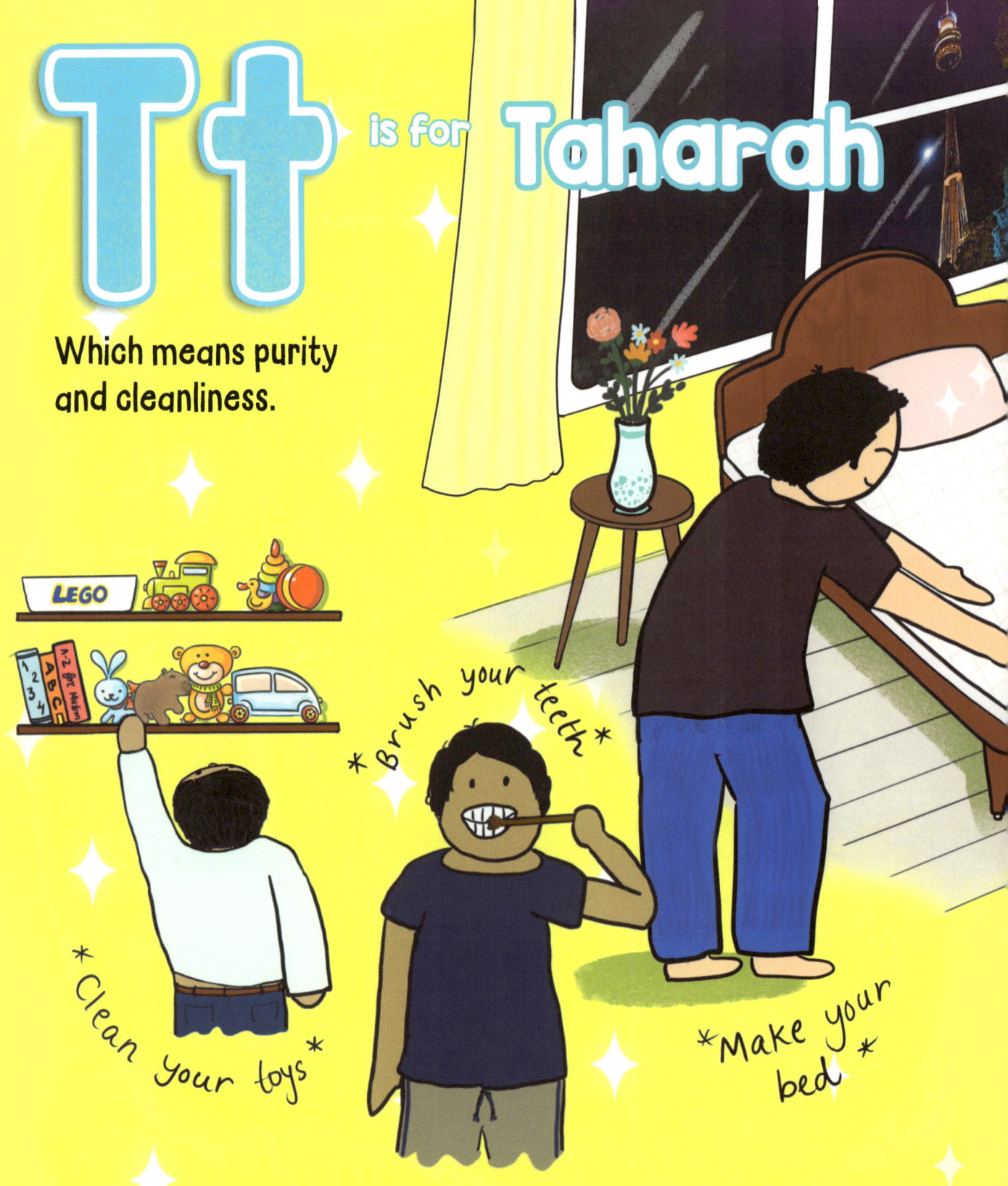

Clean your toys

Brush your teeth

Make your bed

Taharah is an important part of our religion. Being clean signifies half of our faith.

Uu is for Ummah

We are united as one Muslim community! No matter where you are from, we are one, but we are many.

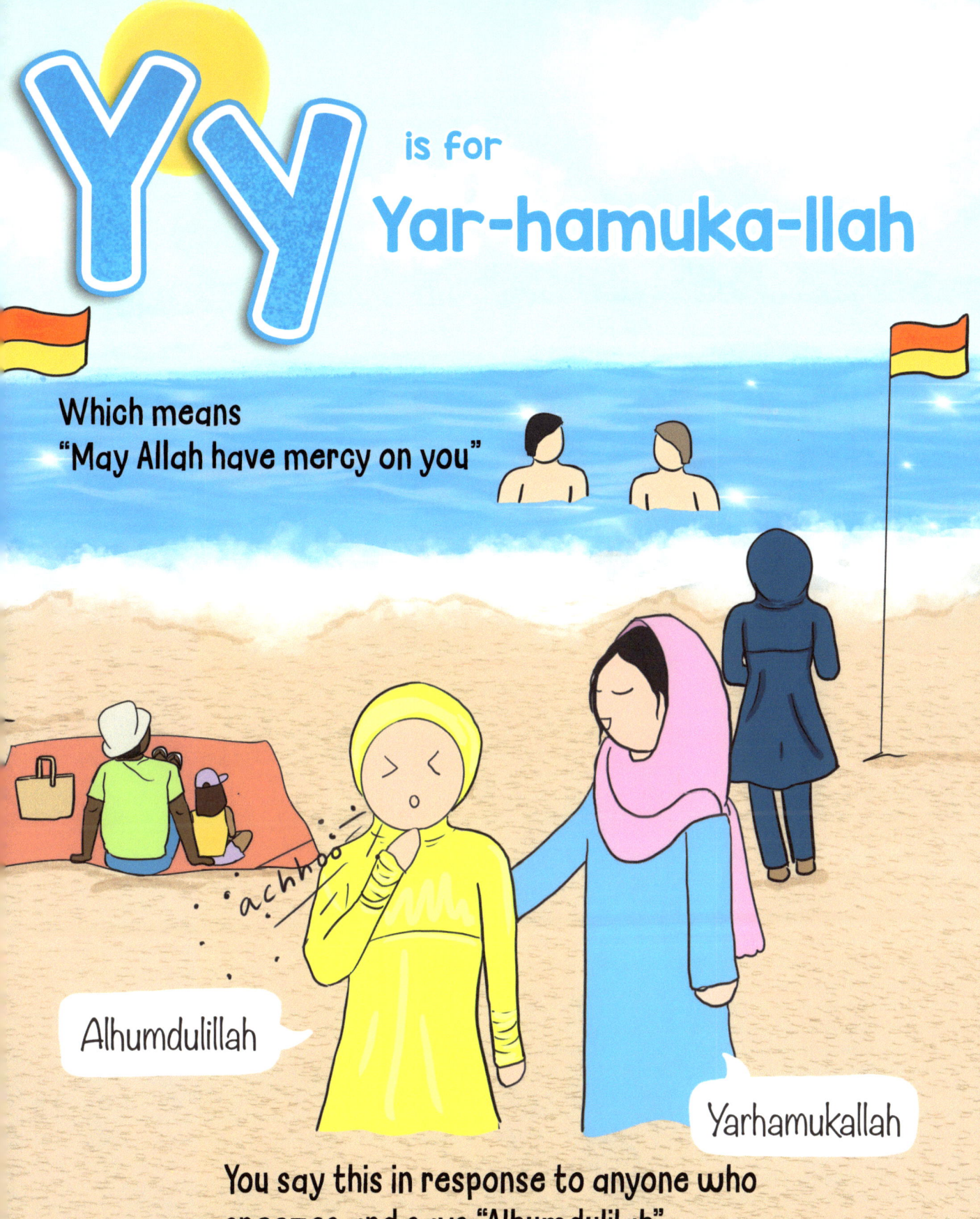

Zz is for Zakah

Which means giving charity to the poor and needy. It is one of the 5 pillars of Islam.

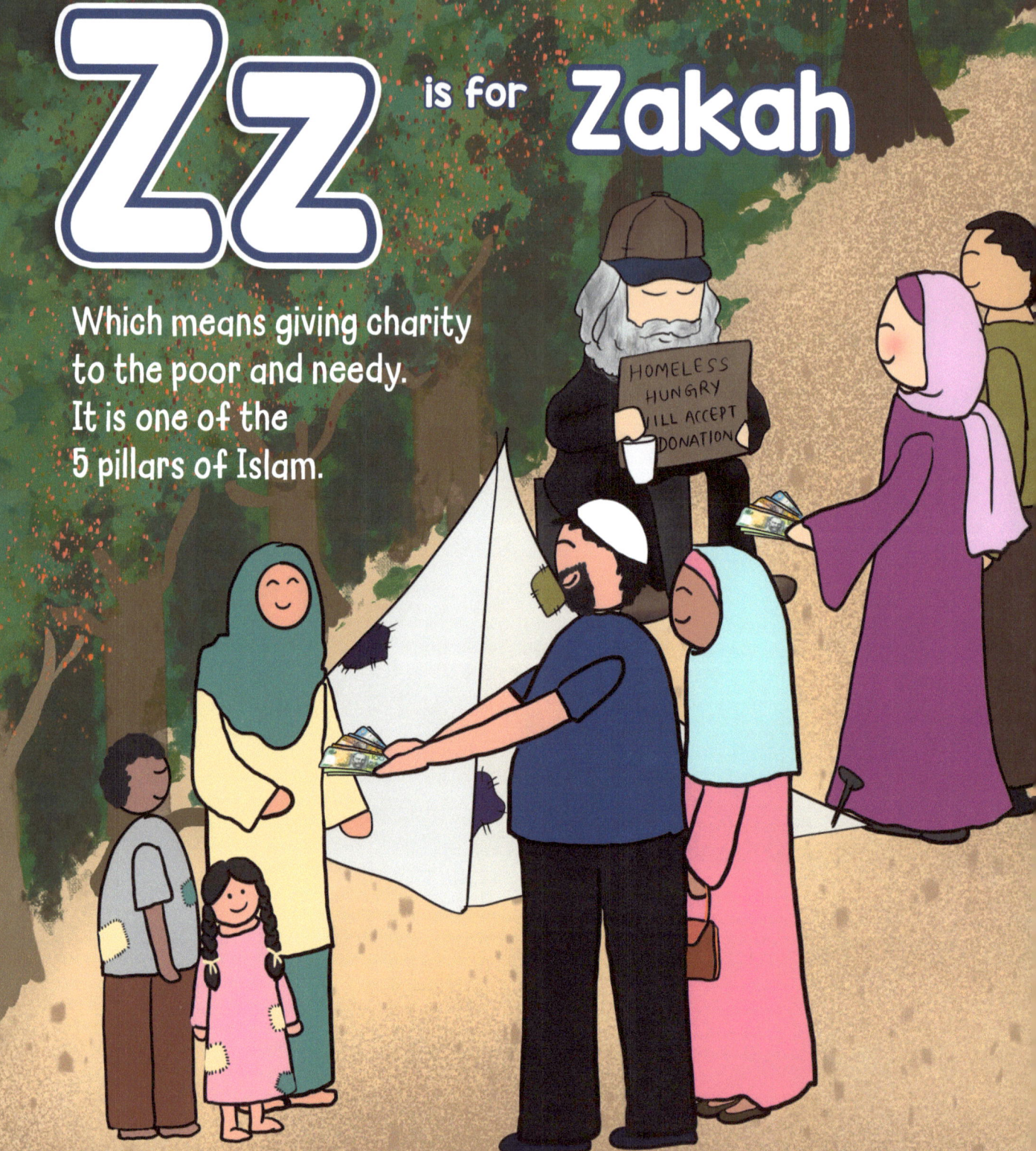

To help anyone in need including the widows and orphans is our duty.

Note to Parents

Please place this book in a safe place to respect the contents of it as it has the name of God and other important words and phrases inside.

In addition, there are millions of Muslims around the world, which for the purpose of these illustrations, not every country could be illustrated (for example in letter Ii). This is in no way intended to exclude or disrespect, however, it shows us that we are all united from around the world as one.

Finally, illustrations have been utilised in a friendly manner for students to explore the concepts of Islam. If you want to learn the steps for certain rituals such as doing Hajj, please consult a professional Hajj handbook for further guidance and advice.

Glossary:

Allah Allah is the name for God in Arabic that Muslims believe in and worship.

Alhumdulilah An Arabic phrase meaning all praise be to Allah. Muslims say this to thank Allah.

Crescent Moon - Islamic months The Islamic calendar has different names for the 12 months of the year.

Dua Dua means to pray (a supplication) to talk to Allah about anything. Muslims make dua when they want something from Allah.

Eid Muslims celebrate Eid (religious festival) two times a year, Eid-ul-Fitr (happens at the end of Ramadan) and Eid-ul-Adha (happens on the tenth day of Dhul-Hijjah).

G'day An Australian word used to greet someone, stands for "good day".

Hajj Hajj is when Muslims visit a place called Mecca in Saudi Arabia to perform a religious pilgrimage. It is the fifth pillar of Islam.

Kaabah Kaabah is a cube shaped building in the middle of a courtyard in the Holy Mosque (the Masjid al-Haram) in Mecca, Saudi Arabia. It is the most sacred site in Islam. It was first built by the Prophet Ibrahim (PBUH). Muslims all over the world face the direction (Qiblah) of the Kaabah when praying five times a day.

Laylat al-Qadr Laylat al-Qadr is a special night where people pray, read Quran and make Dhikr (devotional acts in Islam). It is also called the 'The Valuable Night' or 'The Night of Power.'

Lunar Relating to the moon. Muslims use the Lunar Islamic Calendar which is a calendar based on the monthly cycles of the Moon's phases.

Mecca It is the holiest city in Islam located in Saudi Arabia where the Kaabah is. It is also the place where Prophet Muhammad (SAW) lived before moving to Madinah.

Prophet Is a special person or messenger chosen by Allah to help teach and guide people to do good acts.

Pillar There are five pillars that Muslims follow: Shahdah, Salaat, Fasting, Zakat and Hajj.

Pilgrimage A religious journey. The Hajj, or Pilgrimage to Mecca, is a once-in-a-lifetime obligation for those who have the physical and financial ability to undertake the journey.

Rasulullah Means "Messenger of God". He (Prophet Muhammad Sallallahu Alayhi Wa Sallam) was sent to preach and confirm the monotheistic teachings of Adam, Abraham, Moses, Jesus, and other prophets. He is believed to be the final Prophet of God in Islam.

Salaat (Salah) This means prayer. It is the second pillar in Islam. Muslims pray five times a day from Fajar (dawn), Dhuhr (mid-day), Asr (afternoon), Maghreb (sunset) to Isha (night-time).

Sallallahu Alayhi Wa Sallam (SAW) Means peace and blessings be upon him. Muslims say this everytime after saying the Prophet Muhammad's name out of respect.

SWT When writing the name of God (Allah), Muslims often follow it with the abbreviation "SWT," which stands for "Subhanahu wa ta'ala". This means that All Glory belongs to Him, He is The Most Exalted and The Most High. Muslims say this to glorify God when mentioning His name.

Sunnah Sunnah is the actions and teachings of the way our Prophet Muhammad used to live.

Ummah The whole community of Muslims bound together by their religion of Islam.

Wudu Means ablution or the Islamic act of washing parts of the body using water to prepare for performing prayer and worship.

Zakaat (Zakah) Zakaat is the amount of money donated as charity to the needy and the poor.

Activity: Talking & Listening

A-Z Questions

A - Who is Allah SWT? Did you know Allah SWT created every living thing around us? Can you name some of Allah's creations that you can see?

B - What does Bismillah mean? Can you give other examples of times when we say Bismillah?

C - Have you seen the crescent moon in the sky? Can you draw it in the air? How many Islamic months are there? Can you name them?

D - What are some other duas we can make to Allah SWT? What would you ask Allah for?

E - What is Eid? What do you love about Eid? How many Eids do Muslims have? What are they?

F - What is the name of the month we fast? Do we eat or drink when we fast?

G - What are some ways of being good? How else can we be good?

H - What pillar of Islam is Hajj? Where do Muslims do Hajj?

I - What does Islam teach us?

J - How can we enter Jannah? What good acts can we do to enter Jannah?

K - What does Kaabah look like? Why do people travel to Kaabah?

L - What is special about Laylatul Qadr? What does it mean? When does it fall on?

M - Who is Prophet Muhammad (SAW)? What was he sent with?

N - What can we do to look after our neighbours? How can we be kind to them?

O - What are some of the good/acceptable things we should follow (halal)? What are some of the things we should avoid (haram)?

P - What else can we do to help our parents? How can we show our love and respect to them?

Q - What is the Quran? Who was it sent to? Do you know or can recite any parts of the Quran?

R - What is the month of Ramadan? What kind of things we can do in Ramadan?

S - How many times do Muslims pray? Can you name the five daily prayers?

T - What are some of the ways we can be clean? How else can we be clean?

U - What country are you from? Have you met another Muslim, where are they from?

V - Why should we visit the sick? What dua can we recite when someone is sick?

W - When do we make wudu? What are some of the steps we make for wudu?

X - When have you been excited? What do we say when we are thankful for everything?

Y - What do we say in response to someone who sneezes and says "Alhumdulillah".

Z - What does zakah mean? What pillar of Islam is zakah? Who can we give zakah to?

Acknowledgement

"Read in the name of your Lord Who created. [He] created man [the human being] from a clot of congealed blood. Read and your Lord is Most Generous. Who has taught [knowledge] by the pen. [He] taught man [the human being] what he did not know."
(The Quran – 96:1-5)

I would like to firstly thank Allah (swt) for He made it all happen. Having an idea and turning it into a book is really as hard as it sounds, however it has been more rewarding than I could have ever imagined. None of this could have been possible without the Almighty God's plan.

A special thank you to my beautiful Mum and Dad. I am where I am because of you. I am blessed to have you in my life. Thank you for your amazing love and support throughout my life. Thank you to you both for inspiring me to be the best I can be.

I would like to thank my respected teachers Sheikh Bilal Dannoun and Shaykha Umm Jamaal ud-Din for reviewing my book for approval and authenticity.

Thank you to my beautiful siblings, friends, families, colleagues and community for inspiring me. Thank you to all who I have met and made a difference in my life.

Finally, this book would not exist without my amazing team. I would like to thank the following individuals for making this book become reality: Saba Yasmeen for your beautiful amazing illustrations, Nilufer Kurtuldu and Jackie Hosking for your editing, Praise Saflor for formatting my book and to my amazing colleague Abeer Saleh.

A special thank you to that one amazing individual, you know who you are from supporting me from the moment I had the idea in my mind, to the drafts of my manuscript, giving me advice on the illustrations and cover and always being my number one supporter in life. I am absolutely honoured to have you in my life and will be forever grateful to you. Thank you my love!

Love and peace to you all,
Mariam Latifi
November, 2021

About the Author

Mariam Latifi is a Muslim-Afghan-Australian who loves to educate and has a passion to teach young children. As a teacher, writer and now author of the new book "A to Z of Mini Muslims", Mariam sees a vital need in valuing diversity and promoting religious awareness and tolerance amongst all.

Mariam is an accredited and registered primary school teacher specialising in teaching English as an Additional Language/Dialect. She has worked in many roles including as a Community Education Officer, as a head teacher and as an academic tutor. She strongly advocates bilingual education and passionately promotes a systematic education focusing on holistic learning for school students using current research and pedagogies.

Mariam graduated from the University of Sydney with a Bachelor of Education (Primary Ed) and is now towards the completion of her final semester in her Master of TESOL through Monash University. In the past decade, she has worked in both the private and public sectors across different primary schools throughout Sydney, Australia. Mariam is a wife and a mother to three young girls aged five years and under who love reading. She absolutely loves creating environments for her children to thrive in their learning.

In her spare time, Mariam loves to volunteer and work in her community. She enjoys being the facilitator of a children's playgroup and loves to engage with parents in sharing teaching ideas for developing and promoting children's academic skills.

Growing up as a Muslim and meeting a range of people, Mariam believes in being proud of one's identity and valuing one's own cultural background. This is Mariam's first self-published book inspired by her children, family and community.

Mariam can be contacted at latifi.mariam@gmail.com
www.mariamlatifi.com.au
Instagram (@giftofknowledge) | Facebook (@giftofknowledge)

About the Illustrator

Saba Yasmeen, who goes by her alias as Iqra, was born and brought up in India. She completed her Bachelors in Engineering from the University of Mumbai and later on, to shake things up, she went to Jamia Millia Islamia University, New Delhi to complete her MBA!

She is a self-taught artist, a part time illustrator and a full time dreamer. When she is not drawing she is dreaming about drawing. Apart from illustrating, she takes great interest in learning about cuisines and cultures from around the world.

Saba can be contacted at iqrafty@gmail.com
Instagram- @iqra_fty | @iqra_illustrates

www.ingramcontent.com/pod-product-compliance
Lightning Source LLC
Chambersburg PA
CBHW041428010526
44107CB00045B/1535